S0-ABC-616

Hot Cars

JAGUAR

Lee Stacy

Rourke
Publishing LLC
Vero Beach, Florida 32964

First published by Rourke Publishing LLC.

www.rourkepublishing.com

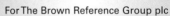

LIBRARY OF CONGRESS CATALOGING-IN-PUBLICATION DATA
Stacy, Lee, 1961-
Jaguar / Lee Stacy.
p. cm. -- (Hot cars)
Includes bibliographical references and index.
ISBN 1-59515-211-3 (hardcover)
1. Jaguar automobile--Juvenile literature. I. Title. II. Series.

TL215.J3S73 2004
629.222'2--dc22
2004013022

For The Brown Reference Group plc

Managing Editor: Tim Cooke
Design Manager: Lynne Ross
Children's Publisher: Anne O'Daly
Production Director: Alastair Gourlay
Editorial Director: Lindsey Lowe

Picture Credits:
IMP AB

Printed in the USA

Some words are shown in **bold**, like this. You can find out what they mean by looking at the bottom right of most right-hand pages. You can also find most of the words in the Glossary on page 30.

Contents

Introduction

The British carmaker Jaguar was started by William Lyons (1901–1985). In 1922 he began a company that made sidecars for motorcycles. By the late 1940s the company also made cars and was named Jaguar Cars Limited. At first Jaguar made mostly sports cars. By the 1960s the company was also famous for sedans and race cars. William Lyons retired in 1972, and for several years the company did not

Jaguar's logo is the head of the big cat of the same name, which is famous for speed and power.

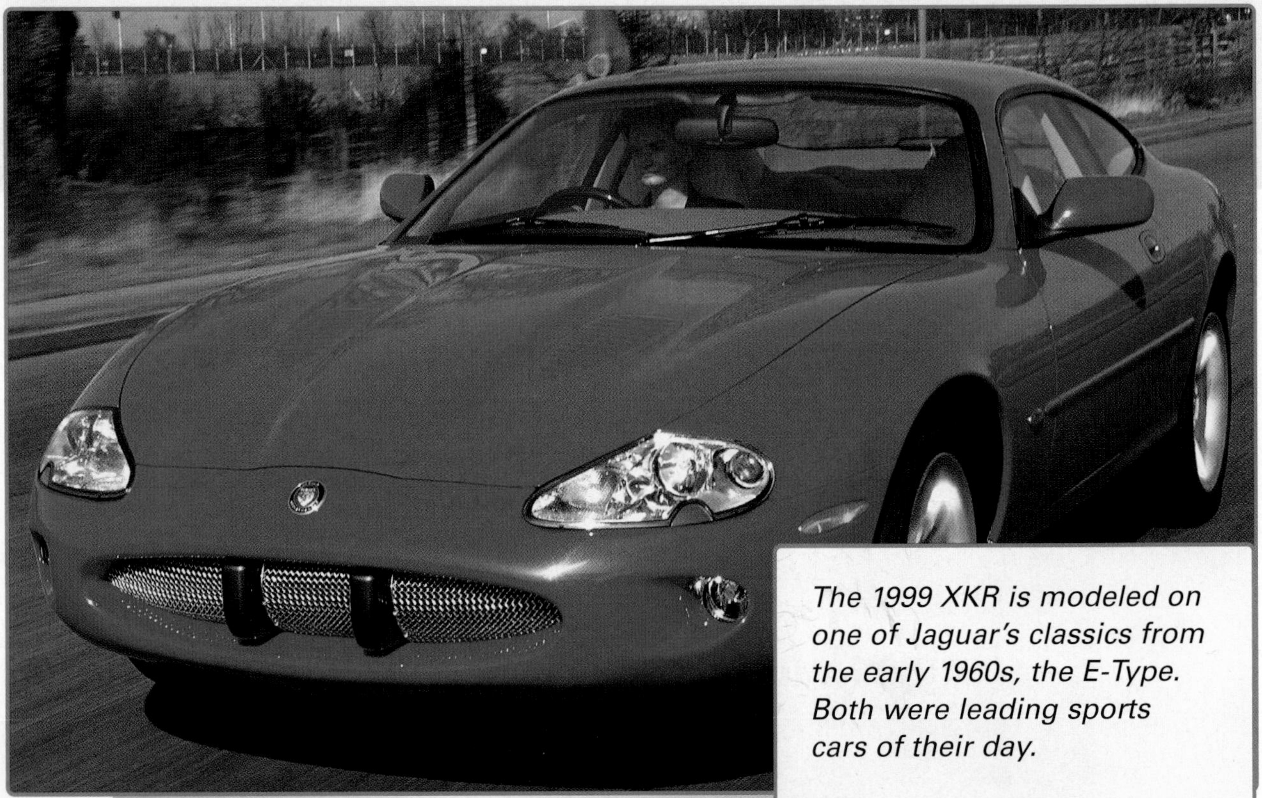

The 1999 XKR is modeled on one of Jaguar's classics from the early 1960s, the E-Type. Both were leading sports cars of their day.

do so well, even though it produced some classic cars. In 1990 Jaguar was bought by the U.S. car giant Ford. Ford's resources and Jaguar's experience of making luxury cars combined to produce some modern classics to add to Jaguar's roster. Some of the company's outstanding models are the E-Type, XJ12 HE, XKR, S-Type, limited-edition XJ220, and the XJR.

Jaguar's XJ220 is one of the fastest sports cars in the world. It is also one of the rarest. Only a few were made in the early 1990s. Each vehicle was assembled completely by hand.

The XJR is one of Jaguar's most popular sedans. It mixes power with style. The engine is a supercharged V8. The interior has both leather upholstery and high-tech gadgets.

Jaguar E-Type

When Jaguar introduced the E-Type in 1961, the public had not seen anything like it before. Critics said that it looked like something from outer space or out of a science-fiction movie. Most agreed that it was sleek and beautiful, however, and performed outstandingly well. When production of the E-Type ended in 1975, more than 72,000 had been built. Today the E-Type is considered one of the great sports cars of all time.

Vital Statistics for the 1961 E-Type Roadster	
Top speed:	*150 mph (241.4 km/h)*
0–60 mph:	*7.3 seconds*
Engine:	*In-line six*
Engine size:	*230.7 ci (3,781 cc)*
Power:	*265 bhp at 5,500 rpm*
Weight:	*2,463 lb. (1,117 kg)*
Fuel economy:	*14.5 mpg*

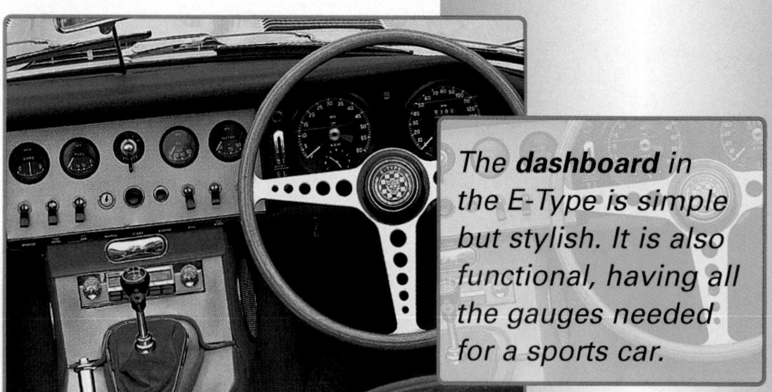

*The **dashboard** in the E-Type is simple but stylish. It is also functional, having all the gauges needed for a sports car.*

Milestones

1961

Jaguar introduces the E-Type at the Geneva Motor Show. The sports car is so popular that Jaguar receives many advance orders from buyers.

1968

The Series II E-Types are given larger hoods and bigger front and rear lights.

1971

The Series III models are launched. Among them is the Roadster with a V12 engine.

1975

Jaguar ends production of the E-Type.

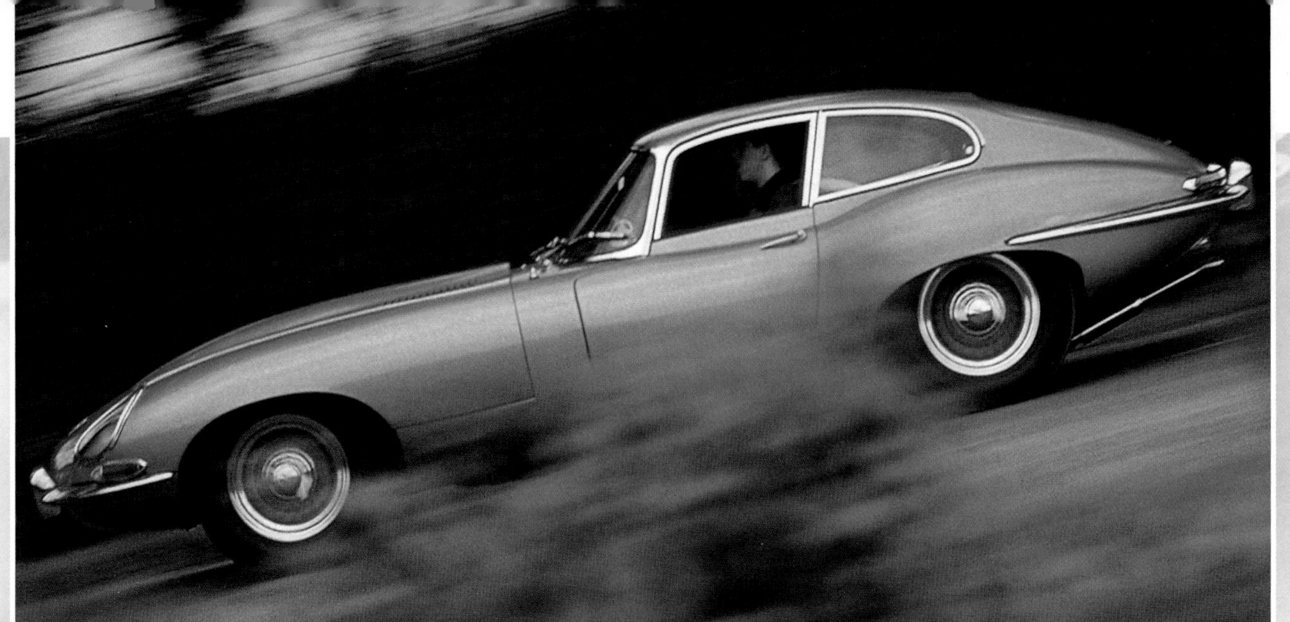

The E-Type is a joy to drive. The view down the never-ending hood promises the thrill of a lifetime, and that's just what the E-Type delivers.

Jaguar produced a lightweight E-Type in 1963. The body was aluminum and the engine was made of **alloy**. Both innovations helped to lessen the overall weight of the car.

Alloy A strong but lightweight metal made by mixing other metals.

Dashboard A panel inside the car that holds instruments displaying information for the driver.

Specifications

Most of the credit for the classic look and outstanding performance of the E-Type belongs to Malcolm Sayer and William Lyons. Sayer specialized in ***aerodynamics*** *and Lyons, the head of Jaguar, was one of the best car designers in Britain.*

Fold-away soft top

The soft top on the E-Type convertible folds neatly away in a space behind the seats.

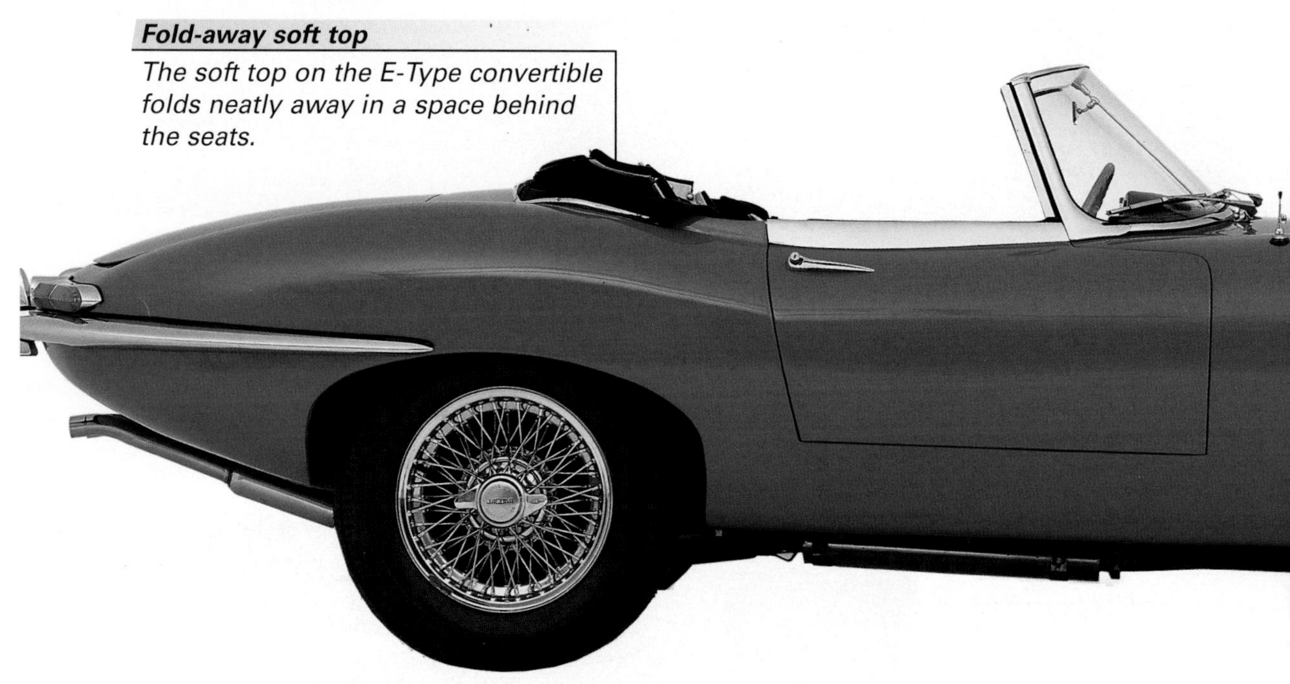

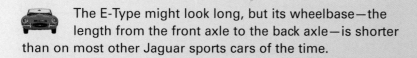

The E-Type might look long, but its wheelbase—the length from the front axle to the back axle—is shorter than on most other Jaguar sports cars of the time.

Most sports cars in the early 1960s had bodies that were supported on a horizontal frame called a chassis. On the E-Type, the body itself, not the chassis, supports the car.

Aerodynamic headlights

Early headlights were covered in hard, clear plastic to make the car more aerodynamic. In the United States, the plastic had to be removed because of federal laws.

Front-hinged hood

The E-Type's engine is very long. To gain access to it, the hood is hinged at the front of the car, near the nose.

Heat vents

The engine produces a lot of heat. The hood has 14 rows of ***vents*** *to let the heat escape.*

Rear suspension

The E-Type was Jaguar's first model to have independent rear ***suspension*** *to give a smoother ride overall.*

Aerodynamics	Designing objects that pass smoothly through the air.
Suspension	A system that supports a car and makes it travel more smoothly.
Vents	Openings that allow exhaust fumes to escape.

Jaguar XJ12 HE

The XJ12 was one of Jaguar's most successful luxury **sedans** of the 1970s. The car used a lot of fuel, however, at a time when gas was becoming more expensive. In 1979 Jaguar came up with a solution: the XJ12 HE. "HE" stands for High Efficiency. The new model performed just as well as the old XJ12 but traveled farther on the same amount of fuel. From 1979 to 1993, when production ended, only a few minor changes were made to the XJ12 HE.

Vital Statistics for the 1985 Jaguar XJ12 HE	
Top speed:	*150 mph (241.4 km/h)*
0–60 mph:	*8.1 seconds*
Engine:	*V12*
Engine size:	*326.2 ci (5,345 cc)*
Power:	*299 bhp at 5,500 rpm*
Weight:	*4,237 lb. (1,922 kg)*
Fuel economy:	*14 mpg*

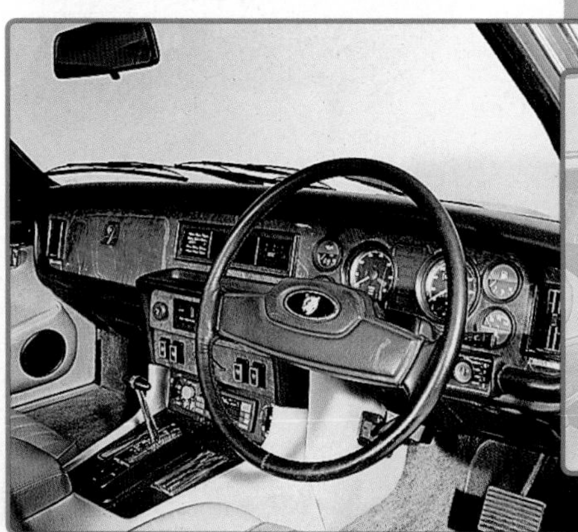

The cockpit in the XJ12 HE is spacious and comfortable. Wooden inlay in the dashboard is a traditional feature of Jaguar cars.

Milestones

1972
Jaguar starts production of the XJ12 sedan.

1979
One of the new models in the Series III XJ range is the XJ12 HE. It comes with a V12 engine adapted from the one used in the Series III E-Type.

1981
After several improvements, the fuel efficiency of the XJ12 HE increases from 13 mpg to 18 mpg.

1993
Jaguar decides to end production of the XJ12 HE.

The change to the new HE cylinder heads made no difference to the extremely smooth and quiet V12, which is matched by incredible refinement throughout.

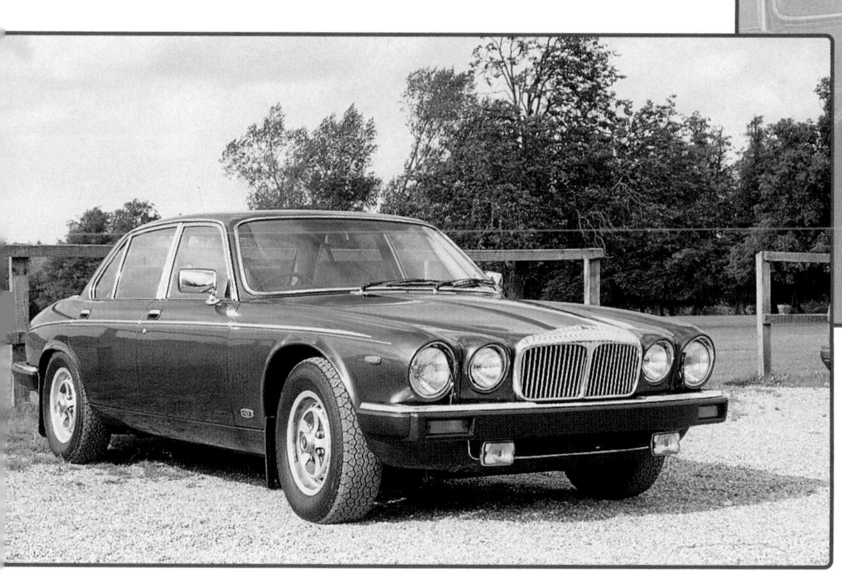

In 1960 Jaguar bought the German car maker Daimler. In the early 1980s Jaguar used the XJ12 body on its own Daimler Double Six model. The only exterior difference between the cars was a new radiator grill.

Sedan A car with two or four doors and seats for four or more people.

Specifications

The exterior of the XJ12 HE is based on the XJ6, an earlier Jaguar classic. The interior is stylish, in keeping with Jaguar's high standards. Under the hood, the engine is a modified V12. Head to head, the XJ12 HE outperformed its competition.

Efficient radiator

To help cool the large V12 engine, Jaguar separated the radiator into a top half and a bottom half. This horizontally divided radiator cools the engine more efficiently.

V12 engine

In the early 1980s, the XJ12 HE's V12 engine was top class. Having two valves per cylinder, the engine created 299 bhp at 5,500 rpm.

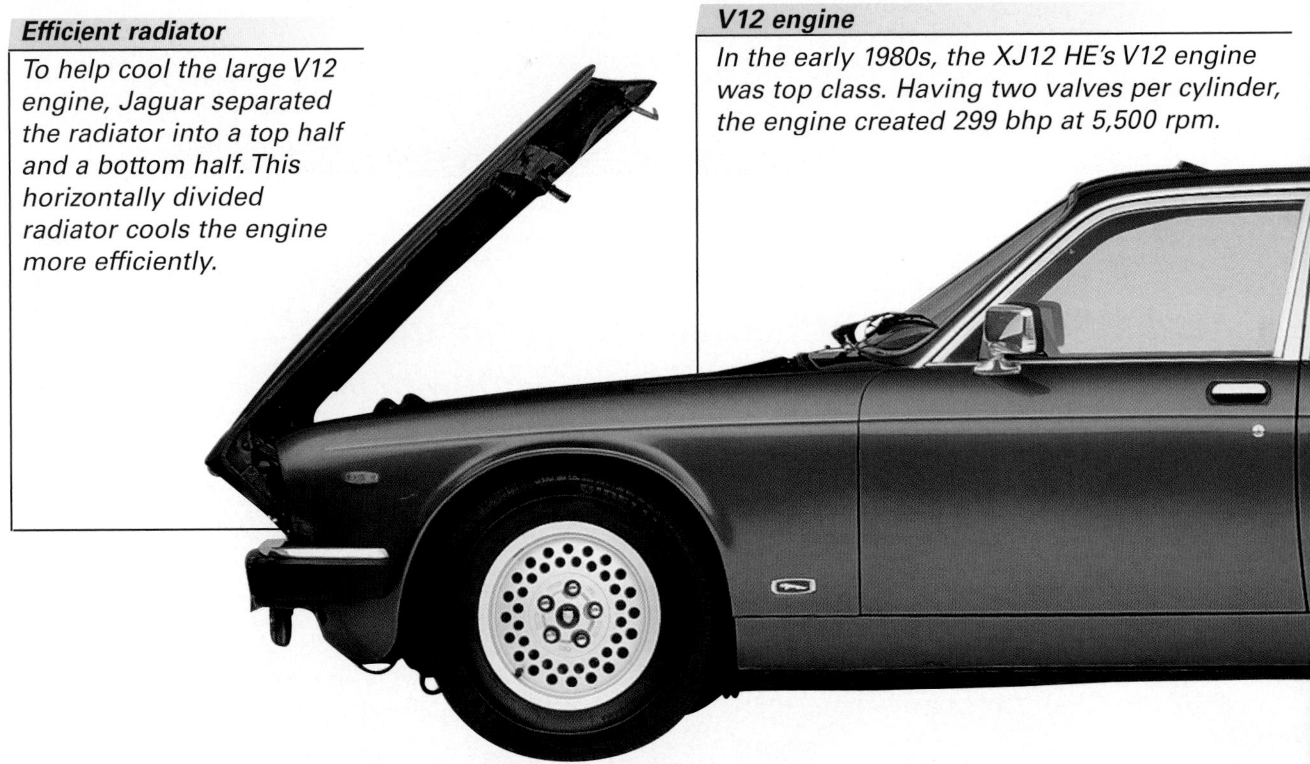

In the first XJ12, the transmission was a poor automatic one that owners complained about. Jaguar's solution was to adapt a much better General Motors transmission for the car.

Another difference between the original XJ12 and the XJ12 HE is the size of the front bumper. The improved model came with a larger bumper that gave more protection.

For turning corners

*To add extra control for turning corners, a limited-slip **differential** has been installed.*

Lightweight alloy wheels

One of the differences between the original XJ12 and the XJ12 HE are the wheels. The first model had steel disc-type wheels. To lighten the weight of the car and to make it more fuel efficient, the XJ12 HE has alloy wheels.

Roomy trunk

Even for a sedan, the trunk is exceptionally spacious. There is plenty of room for the largest type of luggage.

Axle A shaft that runs along the width of the car and on which two wheels are attached. A car has two axles, one in the front and one in the rear.

Differential A mechanism that makes the wheels on either side of an **axle** spin at either the same rate or, for instance, when turning a corner, at different rates to maintain the car's overall balance and speed.

Jaguar XKR

Technically, the XKR is one of Jaguar's most advanced cars. It was one of several 1990s models that benefited from research funded by Jaguar's new owners, the Ford Motor Company. In looks, the XKR resembles Jaguar's older models, such as the E-Type of the early 1960s. Introduced in 1998, the XKR is available as either a **coupe** or a **convertible.** Both versions perform well, but the convertible is slightly less stable because it does not have a hardtop.

Vital Statistics for the 1999 Jaguar XKR	
Top speed:	*155 mph (249.4 km/h)*
0–60 mph:	*5.1 seconds*
Engine:	*V8*
Engine size:	*243.9 ci (3,996 cc)*
Power:	*370 bhp at 6,150 rpm*
Weight:	*3,850 lb. (1,746 kg)*
Fuel economy:	*14 mpg*

Jaguar included the latest gadgets and styling in the two-door XKR. The cockpit is one of the roomiest of any coupe or convertible.

Milestones

1996

Jaguar, now owned by Ford, introduces the XKR at the Geneva Motor Show. It is a critical success.

1997

The XJR is introduced. It has a new type of V8 engine. Jaguar, with Ford's help, plans to adapt the XJR's V8 engine for both the coupe and convertible XKR.

1998

As promised, Jaguar's new V8 engine is included in the latest version of the XKR, along with other changes.

Combining outstanding handling prowess with a soft, supple ride is not easy, but Jaguar has done a remarkable job. It is a refined cruiser of the highest order.

The XKR soft-top convertible is more expensive than the hardtop version, yet critics claim that the ride in the hardtop is smoother and the car easier to control. Despite this, the soft-top XKR is very popular with drivers.

Convertible A type of car that has a top that can be lowered or removed.

Coupe A two-door car that usually seats only two people.

Specifications

The XKR is just one of Jaguar's models to have the supercharged V8 engine. The extra power really suits the convertible, making it perform like a sports car should. To cope with the engine's power, the car has a Mercedes-Benz ***transmission****.*

Supercharged engine

The all-alloy V8 engine has 32 cylinders. The pistons in the cylinders are modified to move more smoothly and to increase engine power.

Front fender

Like the 1960s E-Type, the XKR has an aerodynamic nose and front-hinged hood.

To solve the problem of frost building on the rear window of the soft top, Jaguar offers a removable glass rear window that is electrically heated.

The power and speed are so great on the XKR that the car uses special disc brakes. The brakes are 12 inches (30.48 cm) in diameter. They are vented to release heat and have pads for the high friction created when they are used.

Large rear wheels

The rear wheels are 18 inches (45.72 cm) in diameter, which is large for the size of the car. Big wheels are needed in the rear because the XKR has huge vented ***disc brakes****.*

Power soft top

It only takes 20 seconds for the electrically operated soft top to fold away.

Windshield frame

To support the large windshield, the convertible has a reinforced frame. The frame is also designed to protect the driver if the car rolls over.

Disc brakes A type of brake with a rotating disc inside the wheel mechanism. A clip pinches the discs to stop the wheels.

Transmission The speed-changing gears that transmit power from the engine to the axles.

Jaguar S-Type

The first S-Type was produced from 1963 to 1968. Jaguar brought back the range in 1998, using a combination of Jaguar and Ford parts. The body and interior are Jaguar, but the **chassis** is borrowed from Ford's Lincoln LS. Sedans are generally larger in the United States than in Europe, so the Lincoln chassis makes the S-Type bigger than its European rivals. Its wheelbase—the distance between the front and back axles—is one of the longest on any Jaguar.

Vital Statistics for the 1999 Jaguar S-Type 4.0 V8	
Top speed:	*150 mph (241.4 km/h)*
0–60 mph:	*6.6 seconds*
Engine:	*V8*
Engine size:	*243.9 ci (3,996 cc)*
Power:	*281 bhp at 6,100 rpm*
Weight:	*3,770 lb. (1,710 kg)*
Fuel economy:	*23 mpg*

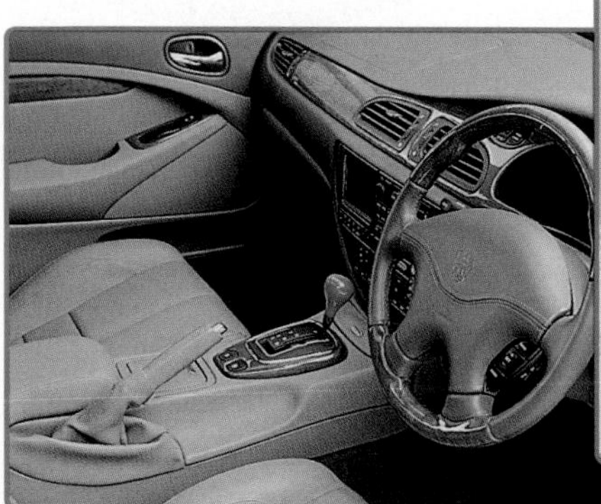

Although the S-Type interior maintains Jaguar's superior standards, some critics argue that it has lost its sleekness and looks more like the inside of a Ford Lincoln.

Milestones

1963

Based on the success of the E-Type sports car, Jaguar expands its range of cars to include a sedan, the S-Type.

1968

The S-Type is replaced with the XJ6 model.

1996

At the Birmingham Motor Show, in Great Britain, Jaguar revives the S-Type but this time it has a Lincoln chassis.

1999

The S-Type is made available around the world. Generally, critics praise the car.

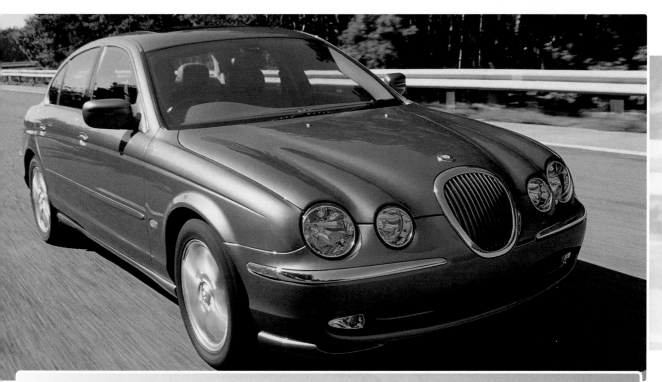

Jaguar's idea to make a true driver's car succeeded. In all respects, this is a Jaguar through and through.

Jaguar offers a choice of either a V6 or V8 engine for the S-Type. The V6 is the economical choice, giving owners better fuel efficiency. The V8 is the more expensive and more powerful option. At top speed, the S-Type with the V8 engine can reach 150 mph (241.4 km/h).

Chassis The supporting frame of the car on which the body is fixed.

Specifications

According to some critics, the revived S-Type is one of the most important cars Jaguar has ever made. One thing that makes it so popular is the way it handles. From front to rear, it is perfectly balanced. Also, technically it was highly advanced when launched.

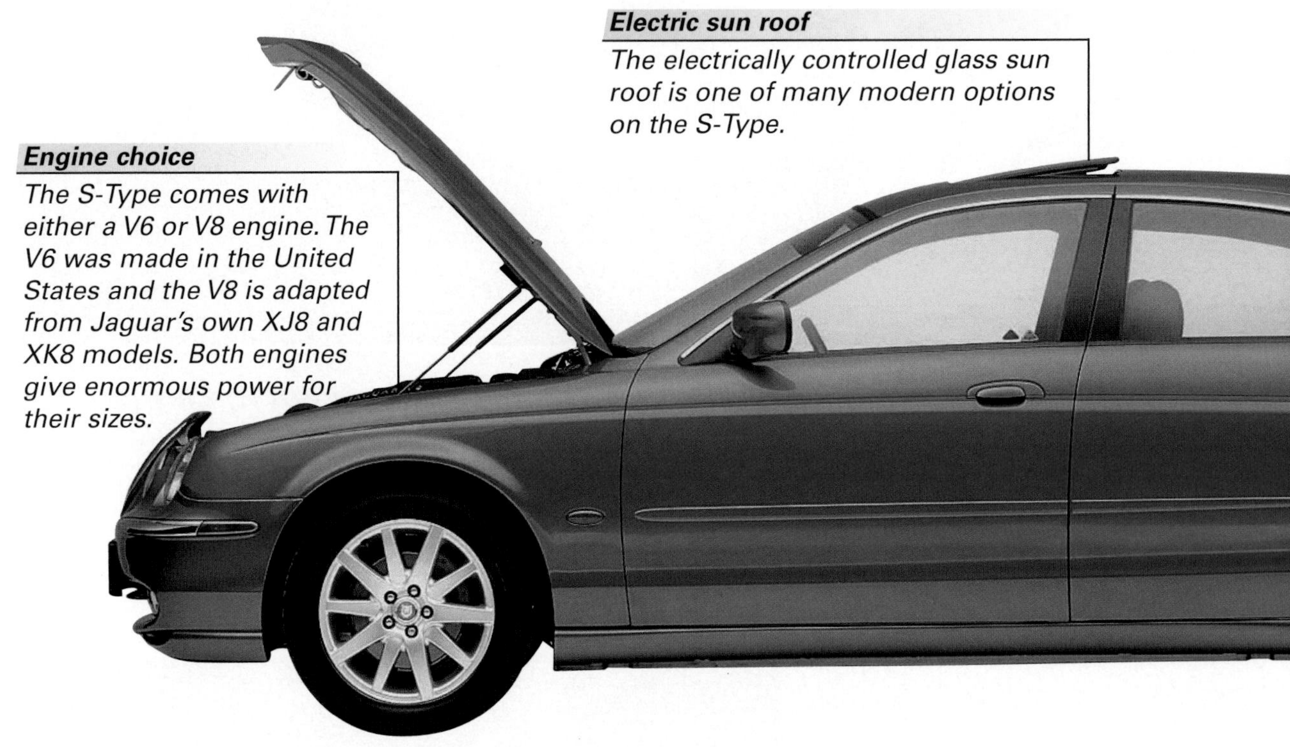

Electric sun roof

The electrically controlled glass sun roof is one of many modern options on the S-Type.

Engine choice

The S-Type comes with either a V6 or V8 engine. The V6 was made in the United States and the V8 is adapted from Jaguar's own XJ8 and XK8 models. Both engines give enormous power for their sizes.

The transmission in the V6 is only available as a five-speed automatic in the United States. Outside the United States, a manual transmission is optional.

As with many modern cars, the S-Type is fitted with rear sensors that give off a warning when the car is too close to another object. This helps to avoid impacts and scrapes.

Lincoln suspension

The S-Type is built on a Lincoln's chassis and ***suspension*** *system. It is a double-wishbone suspension made mostly of aluminum.*

Perfect balance

Jaguar spent many hours making sure the front and rear of the S-Type was evenly balanced. One result of this perfect balance is that the car takes corners easily and smoothly.

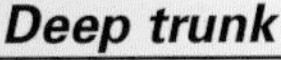

Deep trunk

Because the S-Type has an American chassis, it also has a wide and deep trunk. There is plenty of storage capacity for large luggage.

Suspension A system of springs that support the car on its axles.

Jaguar XJ220

The Jaguar XJ220 is one of the most unusual cars ever built. The car was designed and built by staff at Jaguar in their spare time and without pay. It was a product of love, not a business decision. The Jaguar engineers built it to prove that they could make the fastest sports car in the world. The XJ220 was only in production for two years, and only 281 were built. It cost over $700,000, so few people could afford the car. One belongs to the singer Elton John.

Vital Statistics for the 1993 Jaguar XJ220	
Top speed:	*208 mph (334.7 km/h)*
0–60 mph:	*3.8 seconds*
Engine:	*V6*
Engine size:	*231 ci (3,491 cc)*
Power:	*542 bhp at 7,200 rpm*
Weight:	*3,241 lb. (1,470 kg)*
Fuel economy:	*12.9 mpg*

The dashboard in the XJ220 included what were the most advanced gadgets and instrument panel available in the early 1990s.

Milestones

1988

Designed in secret, the first test version of the XJ220 is shown to the public.

1989

The XJ220 is launched. It has a V6 turbo engine and five-speed manual transmission.

1992

At a track in Italy the XJ220 is clocked at 217.3 mph (349.7 km/h), making it the fastest road car in the world.

1994

Production of the XJ220 ends. Only 281 were made.

The XJ220 is unique, cocooning you in traditional Jaguar luxury. But make no mistake, this Jaguar crouches low like a predator ready to pounce.

Three panels lift up on the XJ220. The front hood exposes the **radiator**. The glass lid behind the driver gives access to the engine. In the rear, the trunk lid covers a small luggage area, just big enough for a couple of briefcases.

Radiator A part of the cooling system that stores liquid that cools the engine.

Specifications

The XJ220 looks quick—and it is. The body is based on one of Jaguar's racing cars from the 1960s, called the XJ13. The speed, over 200 mph (321.9 km/h), comes from the latest in racing technology. The car's only competition comes from Bugatti and Lamborghini.

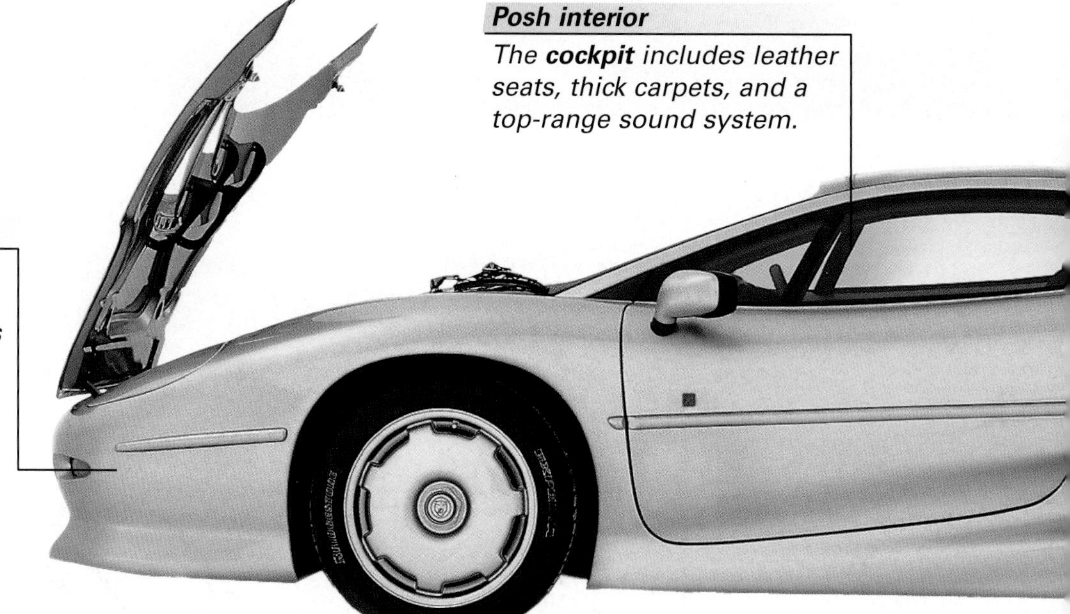

Posh interior

*The **cockpit** includes leather seats, thick carpets, and a top-range sound system.*

Lightweight body

The body is made entirely of lightweight aluminum. The chassis is also aluminum. It is bonded to the body with special adhesive because aluminum cannot be welded.

Each XJ220 was assembled by hand. This took a lot of time, but it one of the things that helped to make the car special. Once finished, each car was painted one of only five colors: blue, gray, green, maroon, or silver.

To help cool the engine there are two sets of vents. Behind the doors, large oval-shaped vents take in air that cools the radiators. On the hood, long curved vents let hot air escape from the engine compartment.

No spare

There is no spare tire. If a tire goes flat, it can be inflated with a special aerosol spray that will temporarily seal the puncture. The tire can then be driven for up to 60 miles (96.56 km) at a top speed of 30 mph (48.28 km/h).

Display glass for engine

The lid covering the engine is glass in order to show off the most important feature of the XJ220.

Hidden headlights

The headlights are lowered into the nose when not in use. This helps the car's aerodynamics.

Cockpit The part of the car where the driver sits.

Jaguar XJR

The XJR is one of the fastest sedans available because of its supercharged V8 engine. Jaguar's superior styling and attention to detail add to its attraction. Capable of a top speed of 155 mph (249.4 km/h), the XJR stands out among its competition, the Mercedes-Benz E55 AMG and the Cadillac STS. One reason for the XJR's power and top performance is that the car's engine and chassis have been adapted from Jaguar's XK8 sports car.

Vital Statistics for the 1998 Jaguar XJR	
Top speed:	*155 mph (249.4 km/h)*
0–60 mph:	*5.4 seconds*
Engine:	*V8*
Engine size:	*243.9 ci (3,996 cc)*
Power:	*370 bhp at 6,150 rpm*
Weight:	*4,075 lb. (1,848 kg)*
Fuel economy:	*19 mpg*

High-tech options, such as a superior music system and fully adjustable seats, help make the experience of driving Jaguar's XJR an unrivaled pleasure.

Milestones

1994

The XJ sedan range is introduced with a powerful six-cylinder engine.

1996

Jaguar's XK8 sports car is the first with the supercharged V8 engine.

1997

The successful XJ sedan receives the supercharged V8 engine from the XK8. The more powerful sedan is named the XJR and can go from 0 to 60 mph (97 km/h) in only 5.4 seconds. The interior and body are also improved.

The only word to describe the seamless flow of power from the supercharged V8 engine is awesome. If you floor the ***accelerator*** *there is instant acceleration on an epic scale.*

Many critics believe that the XJR is one of the finest Jaguars ever made. This is due to its perfect combination of style and power. The supercharged V8 is technically one of the best Jaguar engines, while the interior is top-of-the-range Jaguar.

Accelerator The foot pedal the driver uses to control the speed of the car.

Specifications

Among leading sedans, the XJR is near the front of the pack. Jaguar's skill plus Ford's research budget have created a fast and powerful car. The Computer Active Technology Suspension (CATS) makes sure passengers get a smooth ride.

Powerful and innovative engine

The V8 engine in the XJR was adapted from the XK8 sports car. Its special features include an all-aluminum quad-cam with a modified camshaft that varies the timing of taking fuel into the engine.

Automatic headlights

The headlights have light sensors. When the light outside dims the headlights switch on automatically.

CATS suspension

*To give the smoothest ride possible, the XJR is fitted with the Computer Active Technology Suspension system (CATS). Its suspension system has top-of-the-range **shock absorbers**.*

The XJR's V8 engine produces far too much **torque** for any Jaguar transmission to cope with. To handle the high torque, a Mercedes-Benz S600 transmission is used.

The electronics are highly advanced. The onboard computer processes information rapidly and diagnoses any problem that the car develops.

Luxury interior

As in all luxury Jaguars, the interior of the XJR is extremely comfortable, with leather seats and deep carpets. It is also full of electronic equipment and has a high-quality sound system.

Large rear storage area

The trunk is 14.5 cubic feet (0.41 cubic meters) in size. It is large enough to take several big suitcases without the passengers even knowing the luggage is there.

Shock absorbers Springlike devices that help to smooth out a bumpy ride.

Torque The force that causes an object to rotate. An engine creates torque to turn a crankshaft.

Glossary

accelerator (ek SEL uh RAYT ur): *The foot pedal the driver uses to control the speed of the car.*

aerodynamic (AIR o dy NAM ik): *Designed to pass smoothly through the air.*

axle (AK sul): *A shaft that runs along the width of the car and on which two wheels are attached. A car has two axles, one in the front and one in the rear.*

chassis (CHASS ee): *The supporting frame of the car on which the body is fixed.*

cockpit (KOK PIT): *The area where the driver sits.*

convertible (kun VERT uh bul): *A type of car that has a top that can be lowered or removed.*

coupe (KOOP): *A two-door car that usually seats only two people.*

dashboard (DASH BORD): *A panel inside the car that holds instruments displaying information for the driver.*

radiator (RAYD ee AYT ur): *A part of the cooling system that stores liquid that cools the engine.*

sedan (seh DAN): *A car with two or four doors and seats for four or more people.*

shock absorbers (SHOK ab SORB urz): *Springlike devices that help to smooth out a bumpy ride.*

suspension (sus PEN shun): *A system of springs that support a car and make it travel more smoothly.*

transmission (trans MISH un): *Speed-changing gears that transmit power from the engine to the axle.*

vents (VENTZ): *Openings that allow exhaust fumes to escape.*

Further information

websites

www.cyberparent.com/wheels/jaguar.htm
History of Jaguar

http://auto.howstuffworks.com/engine.htm
How Stuff Works: Car Engines

www.jag-lovers.org
Jag-lovers: A Jaguar enthusiasts' site

www.jaguarusa.com/us/en/home.htm
Jaguar USA

books

- Beck, Paul. **Uncover a Race Car: An Uncover It Book.** Silver Dolphin Books, 2003.
- Buckley, Martin. **Jaguar: Fifty Years of Speed and Style.** Motorbooks International, 2002.
- Sutton, Richard. **Eyewitness: Car.** Dorling Kindersley Publishing, 2000.
- Thorley, Nigel. **Jaguar: All the Cars.** Motorbooks International, 2003.

Index